author's note

Mathematickles! is a brain tickler. It teases your brain by mixing together math and language. Fun words are written in place of numbers in all sorts of math problems—addition, subtraction, multiplication tables, division, fractions, geometry, and more. There are graphs of a snowball fight and an inchworm climbing a branch. Baby-bird beaks become angles and so do twirling seed pods. Just open your mind as the book leads you down a brand new path, on which math becomes fun, silly, beautiful, easy, and creative. You'll find that the seasons tie all the poems together, starting with the first signs of fall and ending with the last breeze of summer. Once you've read this book, I bet you won't be able to resist writing a few math poems of your own.

poems by Betsy Franco + illustrations by Steven Salerno =

Mathematickles!

ALADDIN PAPERBACKS   NEW YORK   LONDON   TORONTO   SYDNEY

crisp air
shadows tall
+ cat's thick coat
signs of fall

nest
- bird
_____
stringfeatherstwigsleaves

squirrels + _____ = winter storage

holes + nuts - nuts = squirrel hide & seek

baskets ⟌ ripeapples / orchard

$$\frac{apples + worms}{sweet\ tunnels}$$

red
orange
gold
+ brown
crunchy rainbow on the ground

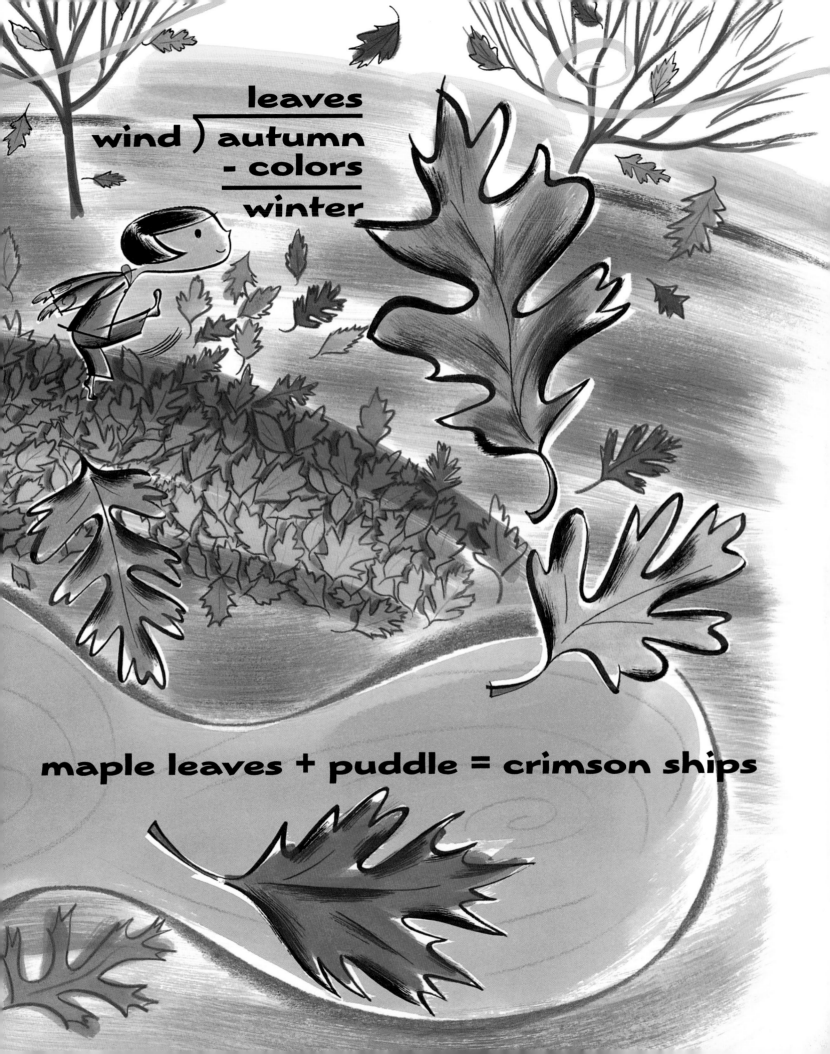

$\frac{1}{2}$ w = v = flying geese

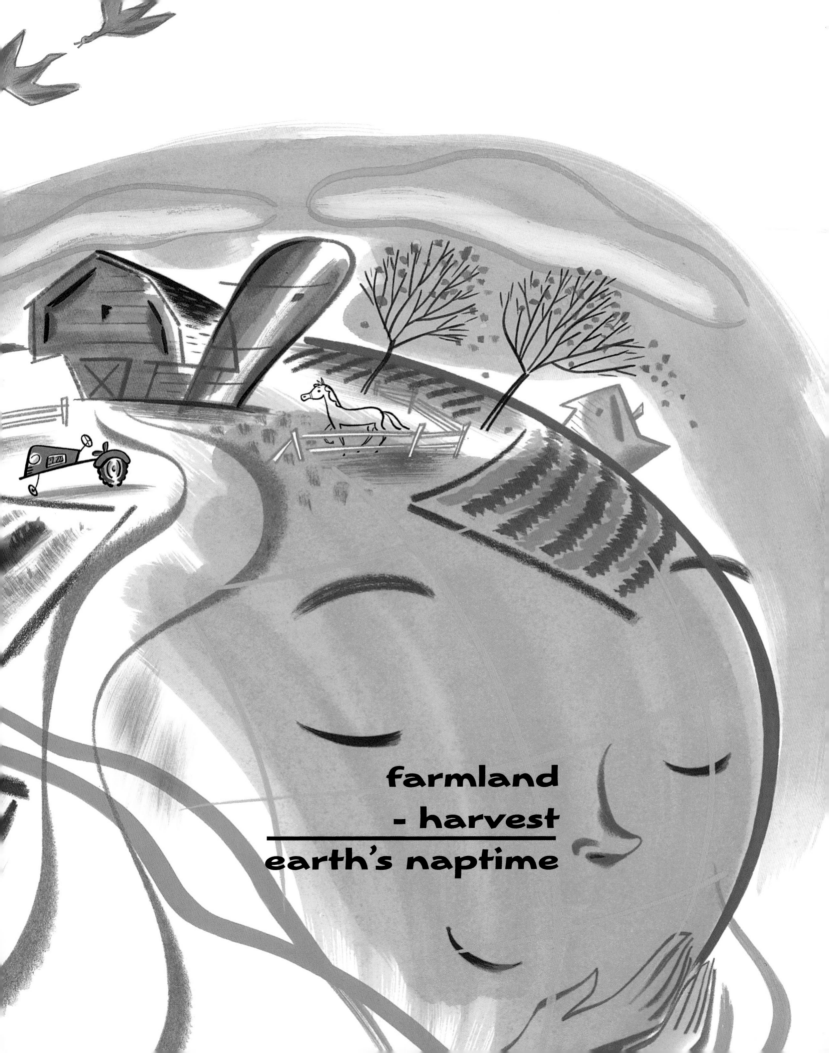

farmland
- harvest
——————————
earth's naptime

$\frac{1}{2}$ of icicle = ice

coldair ÷ breath = tiny cloud

hexagons
$$\frac{\text{hexagons} \times \text{frozen lace}}{\text{snow flurry}}$$

ice puddle + snow boot = creakgroan*CRACK!*

rooftops
+ first snow
white blanket

Preparing for a Snowball Fight

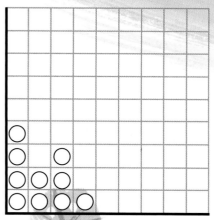

Snowball Fight

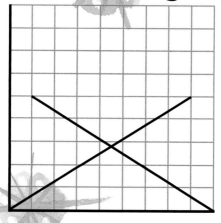

sphere
sphere
+ sphere
---
snowman

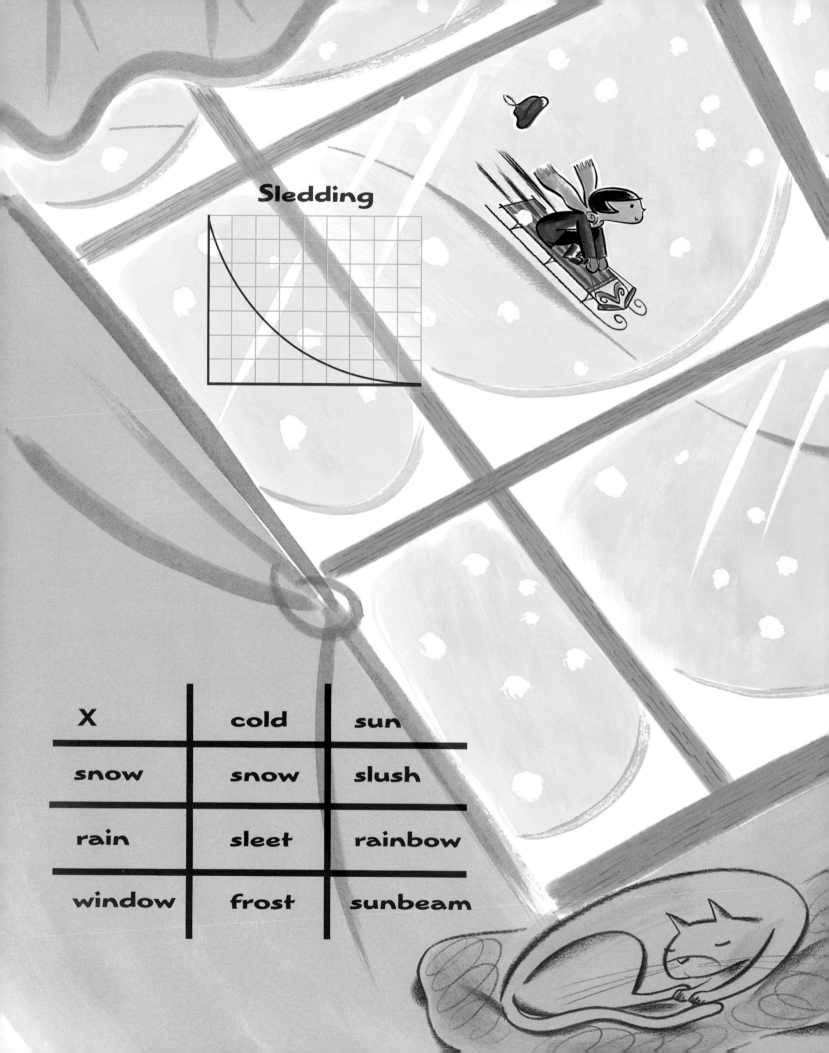

Sledding

X	cold	sun
snow	snow	slush
rain	sleet	rainbow
window	frost	sunbeam

sneeze x 3 = winter sniffles

threads
stitches
triangles
+ squares
-----
winter quilt made with care

$\frac{1}{2} = \dfrac{\text{drip drop}}{\text{drip drop drip drop}}$

tadpole = $\frac{2}{3}$ frog

kitten + leaves + branches - meow = pussy willow

croak
croak
CROAK
+ rrribit
―――――――――
a knot of toads

$$\frac{\text{raindrops} \times \text{leaves}}{\text{pearls on green plates}}$$

Frogs Playing Leapfrog

$$\frac{\text{circles}}{\text{raindrops}\,)\,\overline{\text{puddles}}}$$

baby birds de$\bigvee$ouring worms

Inchworm Climbing a Branch

tulips x daffodils = spring garden

Bird Taking Flight

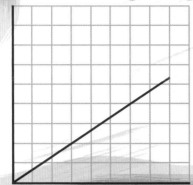

t⌁irling seedpods

Butterfly Dance

clover
+ knots
——————————
springnecklace

pelican diving for fish

$$\text{time}\overline{)\begin{array}{l}\text{waves}\\\text{ocean}\\\text{- rhythm}\\\hline\text{spray}\end{array}}$$

rocks x waves = sand

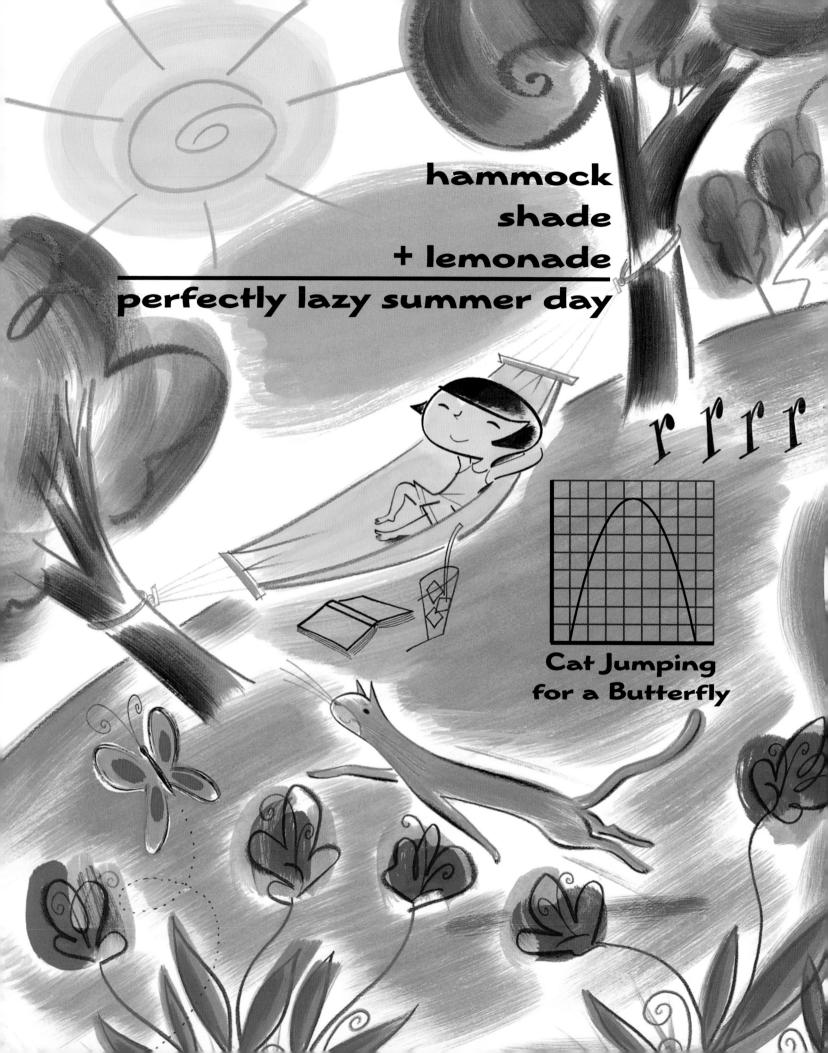

hammock
shade
+ lemonade
─────────────
perfectly lazy summer day

r r r r

Cat Jumping
for a Butterfly

$$\text{lightning} = \frac{2}{3} \text{ triangle} + \frac{2}{3} \text{ triangle} + \frac{2}{3} \text{ triangle}$$

rrummble

BOOM!

$$
\begin{array}{r}
\text{thunder} \\
\text{lightning} \\
\text{wind} \\
+\ \text{rain that's warm} \\
\hline
\text{summer storm}
\end{array}
$$

late summer
x cool air
_____
first fall breeze

soft pillow
sleepyhead
$$\frac{\text{+ clean white sheets}}{\text{time for bed}}$$

lightningbugs x jar = summer lantern

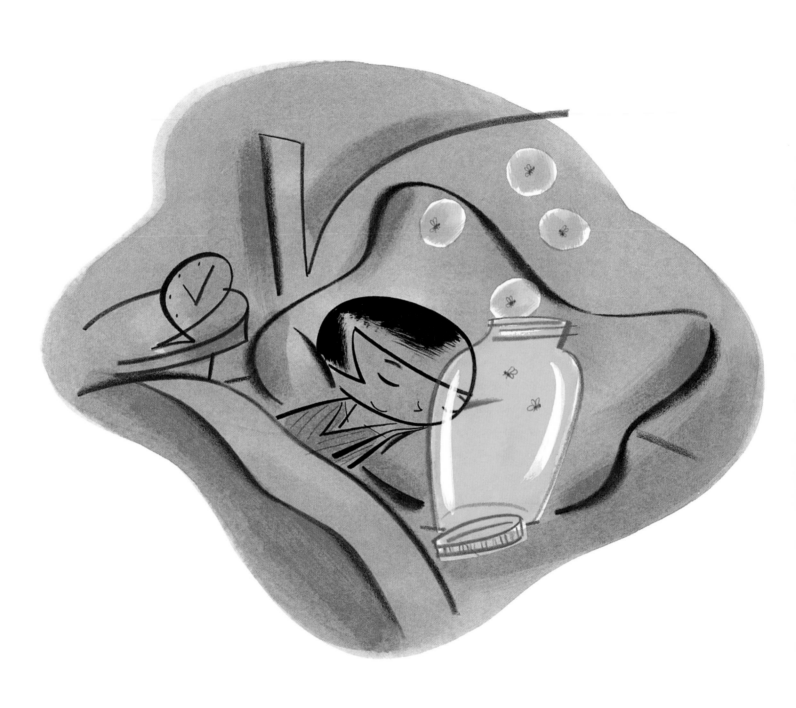

For James, Thomas, and David
I am very grateful to Bob Grumman, whose poetry inspired this collection.
Thank you as well to Justin Ellerby, who helped me brainstorm the title.
—B. F.

For Debby, Christy, Joey, and Tony, and our seasons together
—S.S.

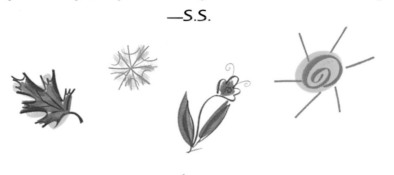

ALADDIN PAPERBACKS

An imprint of Simon & Schuster Children's Publishing Division

1230 Avenue of the Americas, New York, NY 10020

Text copyright © 2003 by Betsy Franco

Illustrations copyright © 2003 by Steven Salerno

Also available in a Margaret K. McElderry Books for Young Readers hardcover edition.

Designed by Sonia Chaghatzbanian.

The text of this book was set in Havergal.

The illustrations for this book were rendered in watercolor and gouache.

Manufactured in China

10

The Library of Congress has cataloged the hardcover edition as follows:

Franco, Betsy.

Mathematickles / Betsy Franco ; illustrated by Steven Salerno.

p. cm.

Summary: A collection of poems written in the form of

mathematical problems and grouped according to seasonal themes.

ISBN 978-0-689-84357-0

1. Mathematics—Juvenile poetry. 2. Children's poetry, American. [1. Mathematics—Poetry.

2. Seasons—Poetry. 3. American poetry. 4. Visual poetry.] I. Salerno, Steven, ill. II. Title.

PS3556.R3325 M37 2003

811'.54—dc21

2001055844

ISBN-13: 978-1-4169-1861-5 (pbk.)

ISBN-10: 1-4169-1861-2 (pbk.)

0118 SCP